ANIMAL
BONES

ISBN: 978-0-9838923-1-1

For what's-yer-face.

ANIMAL BONES

by Gary Bueno

www.garybueno.com

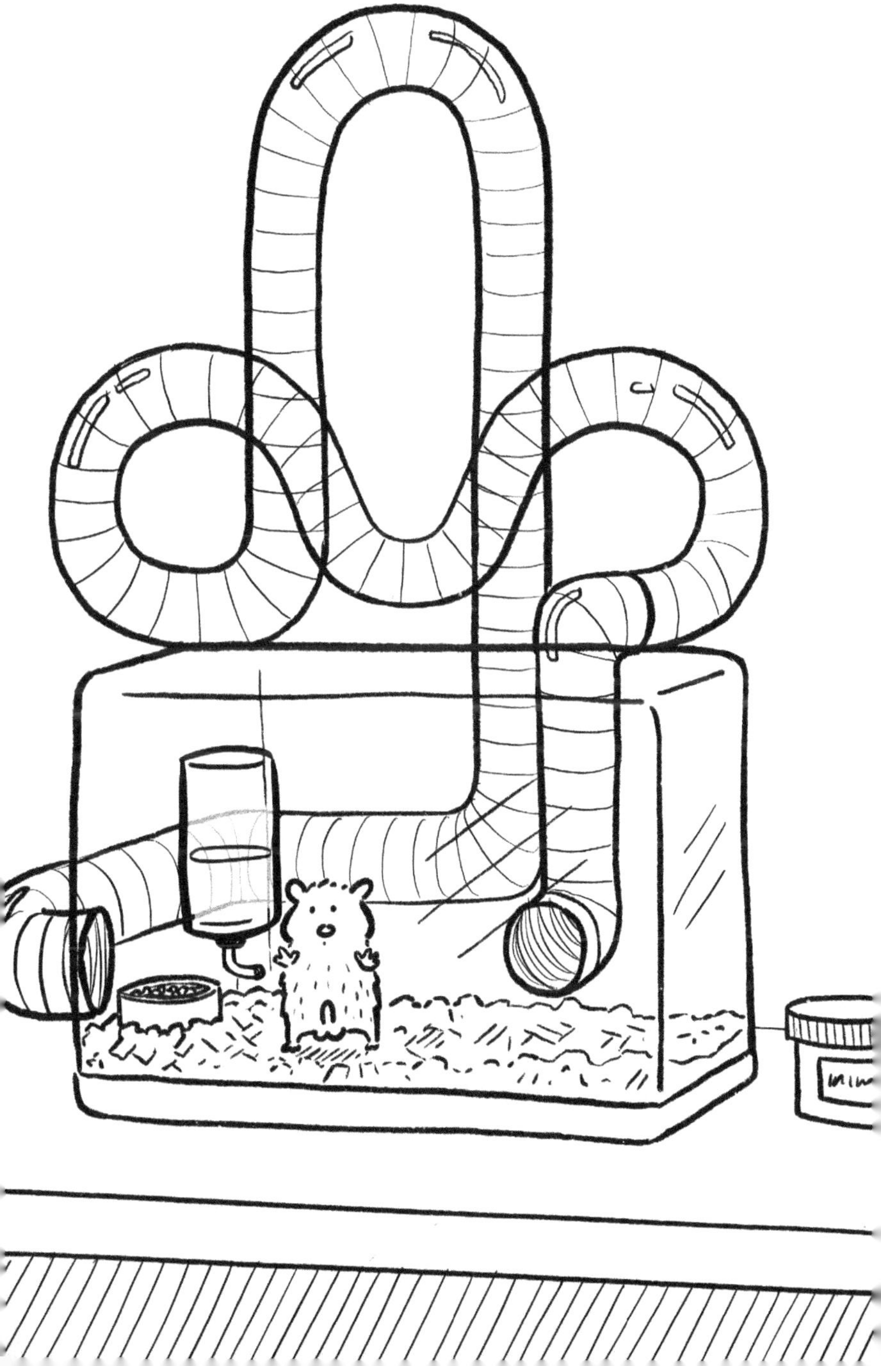

W
N
S
E

CIRCUS

FLEA CIRCUS

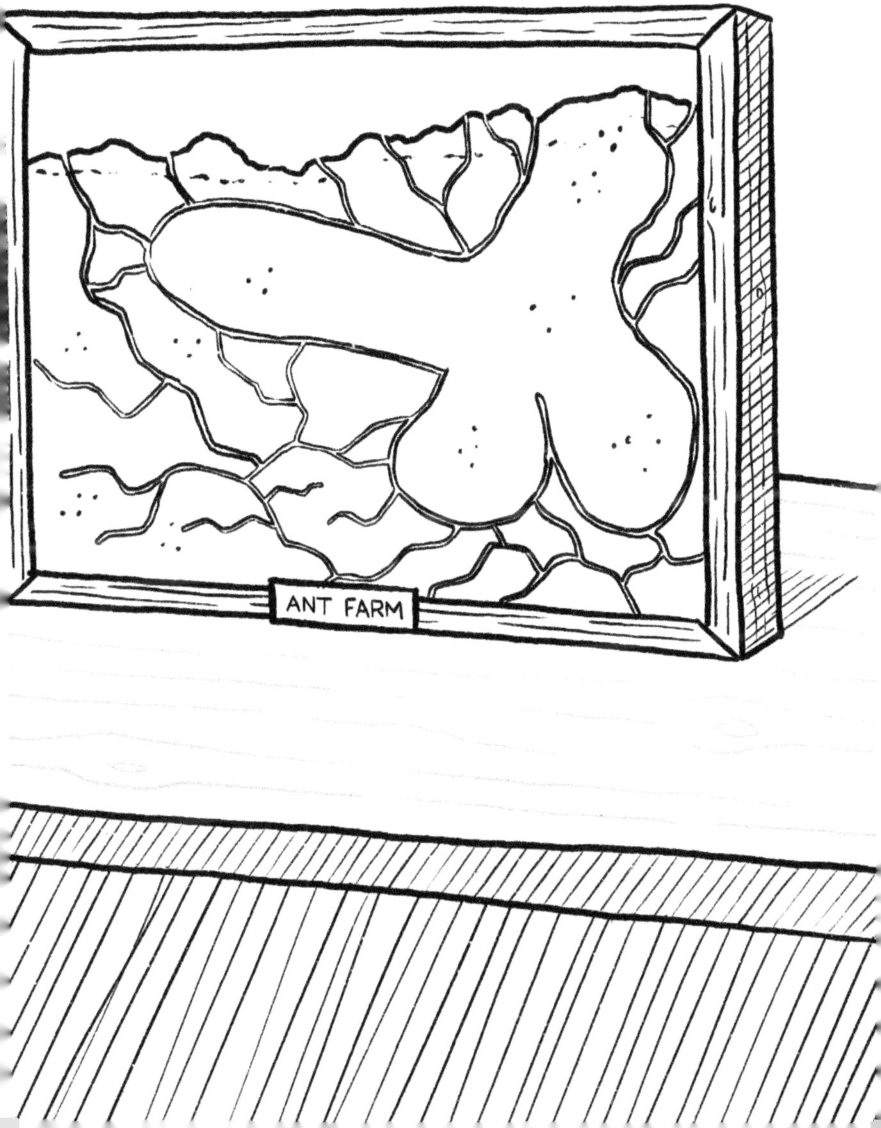
ANT FARM

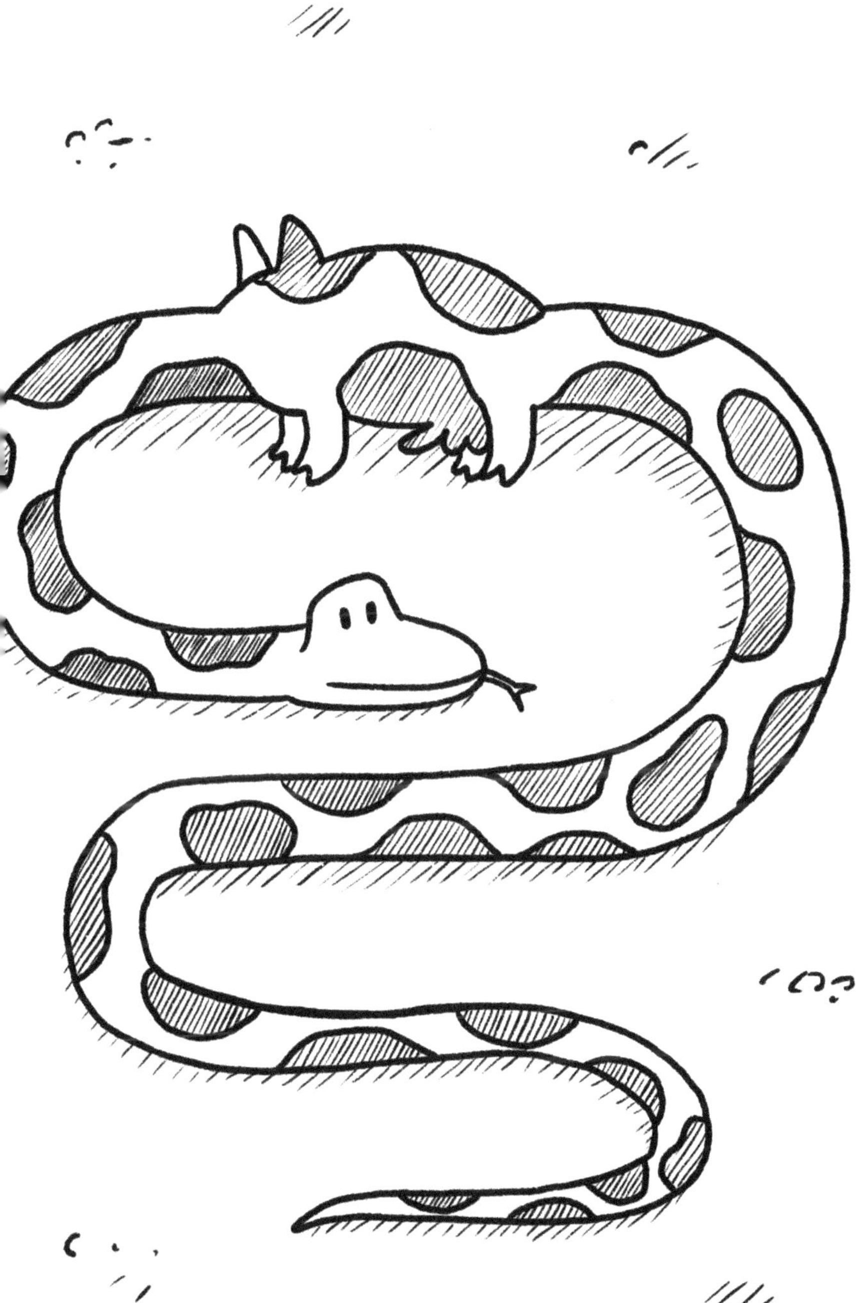

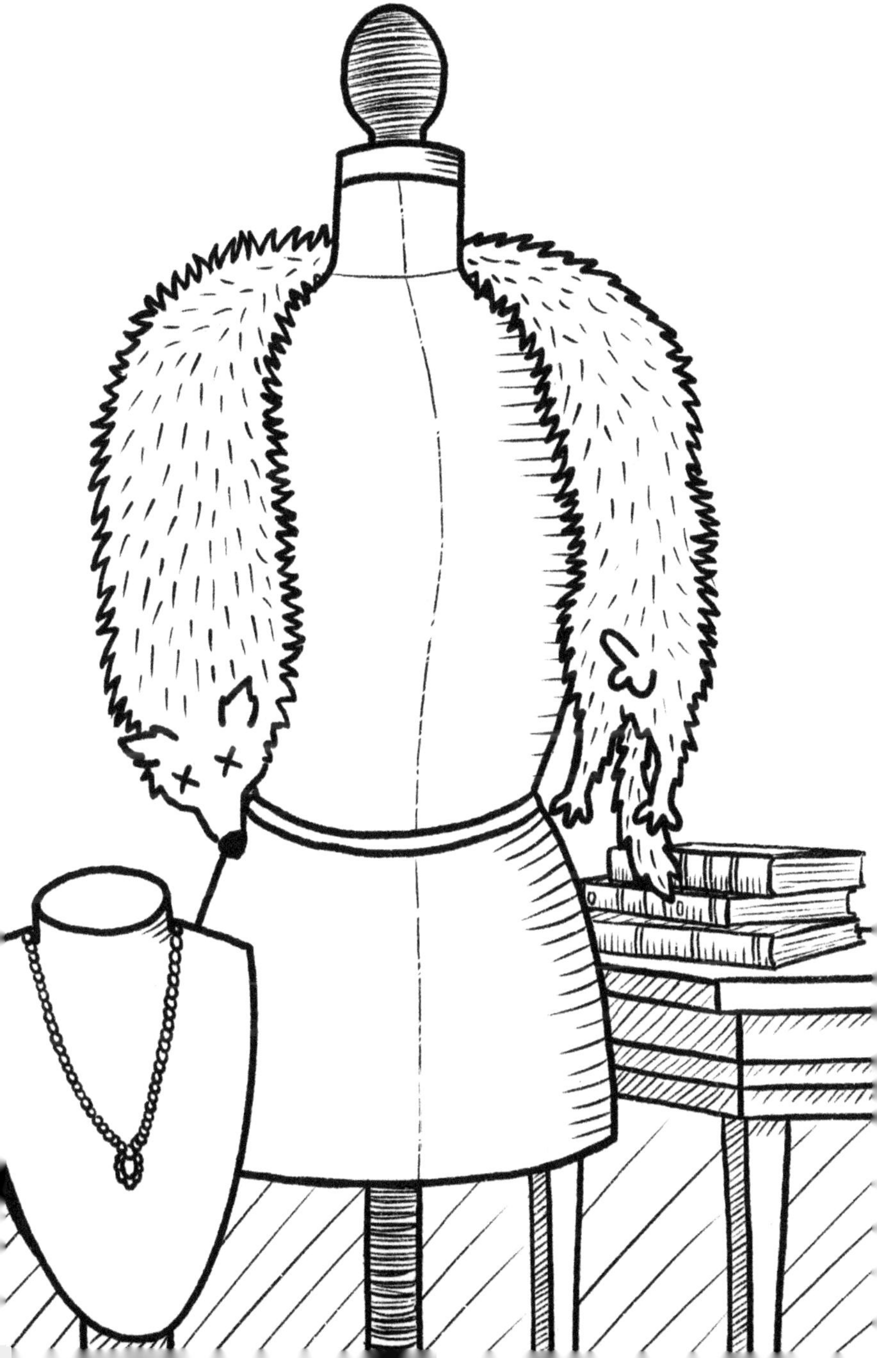

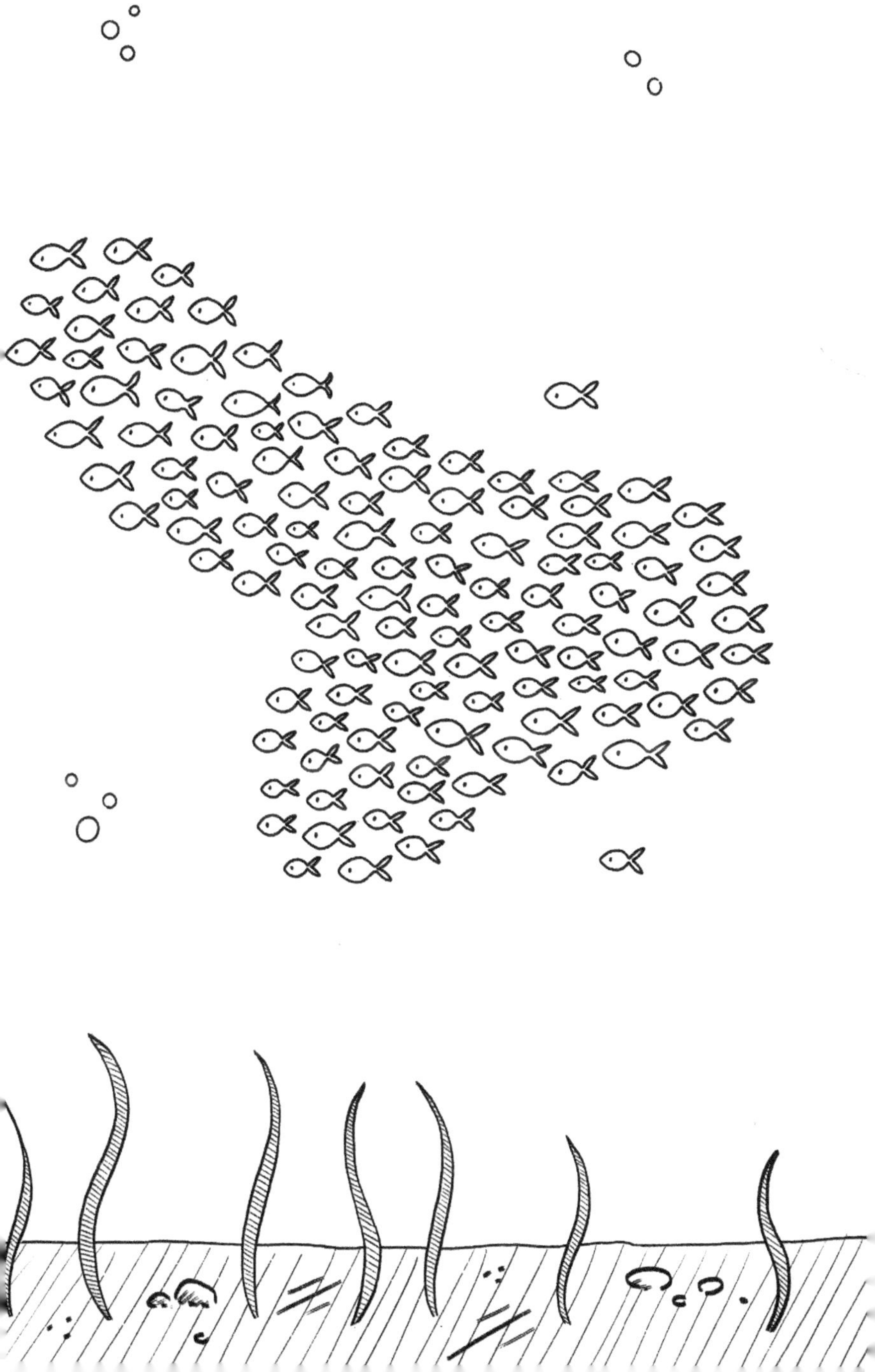

PHIN
龟 TURTLE
熊猫 PANDA
狼 WOLF
獭 OTTE
SHARK
虎 TIGER
犀牛 RHINO
海牛 MANATEE
麝牛 MUSK OX
斑马 ZEBRA
美洲虎 JAGUAR

HAVE YOU SEEN THIS DOG?
REWARD:

www.ingramcontent.com/pod-product-compliance
Lightning Source LLC
Chambersburg PA
CBHW071622040426
42452CB00009B/1451
9780983892311